THE MILLIONAIRE FIREFIGHTER

THE MILLIONAIRE FIREFIGHTER
How First Responders Can Create Extraordinary Wealth From an Ordinary Income
Copyright © 2023 Greg Clatterbuck

Paperback: 978-1-964046-51-8
Kindle: 978-1-964046-53-2

Expert
Press
www.ExpertPress.net

Expert Press
2 Shepard Hills Court
Little Rock, AR 72223
www.ExpertPress.net

Editing by Chelsea Morning
Copyediting by Heidi Ward
Proofreading by Abby Kendall
Text design and composition by Emily Fritz
Cover design by Casey Fritz

THE MILLIONAIRE FIREFIGHTER

HOW FIRST RESPONDERS CAN CREATE
EXTRAORDINARY WEALTH
FROM AN ORDINARY INCOME

GREG CLATTERBUCK

CONTENTS

INTRODUCTION

IF YOU'RE A FIRST RESPONDER or frontline worker, you may feel skeptical seeing the words "millionaire" and "firefighter" in the same sentence, let alone as the title of a book. That's because people like us—the firefighters, police officers, EMTs, paramedics, nurses, and teachers of the world—just don't tend to make the kind of salary that catapults us to millionaire status.

But what if I told you that I—someone who has been a full-time, career firefighter for twenty years—have achieved that status?

Your gut reaction might be to not believe I could make millions of dollars on a firefighter's salary. And you know what? That reaction is absolutely right. I can't, and I haven't. Yet I've still managed to build myself a net worth of over one million dollars. But I promise, I'm not sharing this information with you to brag. I'm sharing it with you for exactly the opposite reason: I want you to be able to say the same thing about yourself. I want you to achieve millionaire status too.

In fact, I don't just *want* you to achieve that feat—I *know* you can. Because whether you're a first responder, a blue-collar worker, or just someone who makes less money than you would like to in the career you've chosen, I'm telling you that if I can find a way to get there, so can you. And no, it doesn't involve going back to school or making a total career shift. It just involves a willingness to figure out how you can supplement your income in a way that also allows you to keep doing the work you've come to know and love.

For me, investing in real estate made achieving that goal possible.

I'm still a full-time firefighter. And I still run a home-inspection business on the side called Clatterbuck Home Inspections. But even with those two jobs taking up more than seventy hours of my time each week, I manage to invest in real estate regularly and build my wealth beyond anything my "normal" jobs would ever be able to provide me with. That's because I've spent years honing the skills it takes to invest well, to manage properties well, and to bring investors into the fold who also want to benefit from the kind of work I'm doing. Most importantly, I've learned from others in my field so others can learn from me.

And now my goal is to share the opportunity to do the same with you. But the beauty of this book is that, thanks to the knowledge within, you won't have to spend years and years to get where I am. Instead, you'll have a leg up on the process of understanding what real estate investing is, what it takes to do it successfully, and what your options are.

However, it's also important to understand that *The Millionaire Firefighter* is not your traditional "how-to" book. Yes, this book will teach you some of the basics every first-timer needs to know about what it means to invest in real estate. I'll even share details about opportunities for those who want to invest but may not be interested in doing all the start-up work that comes with purchasing and managing rental properties.

Even so, though the pages of this book contain valuable information and insights, by and large, I've deliberately avoided making it a strict how-to book for two reasons. The first is that there are a million different how-to books out there about investing in real estate. I've read a bunch of them, and they're great resources that I highly recommend exploring. But I didn't want my book to be just another how-to book that gets tossed into your I'll-get-to-it-someday pile.

The second—and more important—reason is that I wanted to make this book a universally useful resource for anyone at any stage of their life or career, and strict, step-by-step how-to books tend to not check that box. That's because writing a carefully guided how-to book for someone requires knowing exactly what how-to (or goal) that person is looking to achieve and exactly what means they have to get there. Sure, I could say I'm writing a book about "how to become a millionaire," or even "how to invest in real estate," but what exactly would that look like? What kinds of steps could I possibly put in either of those books that every reader, no matter their background or status, could apply in the same way? The reality is, a how-to book is only useful if the person reading it knows exactly what path they want to walk in order to achieve a very specific end goal.

So *The Millionaire Firefighter* is not a how-to book. Instead, it's meant to inspire you to see that there are options you can implement to build your wealth and that all it comes down to is having the right mindset and attitude when going about it. And this book does that by using real estate investing as an example of that fact because, based on my own experience, real estate proves time and again to be an option that's truly feasible for *anyone* to explore and use to build wealth. By sharing my personal mindset, stories, and expertise with real estate investing, I'm hoping you'll see just how achievable millionaire status really is—even if you currently know nothing about investing in real estate.

And trust me, I knew next to zero about real estate when I set out on my own path. All I knew was that I needed to find a way to start building wealth. I had no idea where to start. At least, not until I began to understand that "being wealthy" is an entirely subjective term. In other words, it changes shape and meaning for every person, because each of our lives has different requirements and desires based on factors like where we live, the size of our family, the work we do, the hobbies we enjoy—you name it. What we want out of life greatly impacts what we believe it means to be "wealthy."

That being the case, what does wealth look like to you? Does it mean owning five yachts and taking a European vacation every other week? Or does it simply mean not having to worry about how you're going to feed your family if you suddenly have to pay to replace a broken water heater?

For me, being wealthy means not living paycheck to paycheck. It means having enough money in the bank to not worry about how I'm going to pay all my bills *and* pay for emergencies if they come up. In fact, it means that expenses like a broken HVAC, a water heater, or tires on my car aren't considered emergencies and I can instead treat them as planned life events according to the lifespans of those items. Being wealthy also means being able to take my family on vacation a few times a year. And it means feeling confident that after I'm gone, my daughter will find support in what I've left behind for her, both in finances and in an education she can use to her own advantage.

I consider myself wealthy not because of the amount of money I have but because of the kind of life that money allows me to live: a comfortable one that makes it so that I don't have to think about money all the time.

If you're not sure what wealth looks like for you or how to go about putting those ideas together, start by thinking about building wealth like buying a car. When you're shopping for a new car, you have to consider what kind of car suits your needs. Do you need a truck for hauling cargo? Or maybe just a simple sedan to commute to and from work? Or do you need a three-row SUV to transport your entire family at once? When you shop, you pick the kind of vehicle that not only gets you where you want to go but does so in the manner your unique circumstances require for getting there. And building wealth is the same. You have to pick the vehicle that best suits your circumstances and destination by under-standing what you should do *now* in order to get where you want to go *later*.

And that brings us back to considering how real estate can be the vehicle you need. In my experience and the experience of those I work with and learn from in the industry every day, no matter where you find your finances have taken you thus far, there are ways to use real estate to help you build your wealth. It's a truly fantastic option for so many people to explore because there are so many different ways to go about it—no matter what your current day job or salary might look like.

If you'd like to see the proof in that statement while learning a little bit about how it's possible along the way, you've come to the right book. My goal is to use my story and experience to show you that anyone can do this. Anyone can become a millionaire firefighter, police officer, paramedic, or blue-collar worker. Anyone can build the wealth they want if they're ready to embrace what that means and be open-minded about how to get there.

All it takes is finally deciding to get started. So stop dreaming about trying something someday. Stop wondering how things might be different if you decided to make some plans. And stop putting those plans off because you're not sure how things will work out.

How do you eat an elephant? One bite at a time. You just have to start!

CHAPTER ONE
I'M JUST LIKE YOU

DEPENDING ON HOW YOU CAME to find this book, you might have heard my name or maybe heard about my business. But beyond that, you probably don't know much about me. To you, so far, I'm just some guy who's apparently a firefighter and a home inspector and a real estate investor all wrapped into one.

If I'm going to relay my experiences to inspire you and ask you to trust me enough to believe that what I'm sharing with you is accurate and achievable, I owe you a little background. But more than that, I owe it to you to prove I am just like you. I started in the same or in a similar place to where you are likely starting, and I've accomplished things I never used to think were possible. And though I've already said it once, I'll say it again: If I can do it, so can you.

I'll start by saying that in the scope of living the "American Dream," I'm a pretty average Joe. I grew up an only child in rural Virginia with my parents. My dad worked for the Department of Transportation and also operated our small family farm, while my mom worked for Virginia Cooperative Extension (providing education services for farmers). Most of the families in my small town were also comprised of farmers and blue-collar workers. My high school was the only one in the entire county, and my graduating class only had 120 students. We didn't get our first McDonald's until I was in eleventh grade. I even remember as a kid asking what an entrepreneur was and being told it was "just a shady businessperson."

In many ways, that might make me seem "below average," but my family lived comfortably. We were by no means rich, but my parents made enough money raising and selling cattle and working full time that we didn't want for much. I was a happy kid who played football, helped with the farm on weekends, and always looked forward to the first day of hunting season. That was the kind of community I grew up in, and everyone in town who was my age lived similarly.

But what I think set us apart from young adults living in the city were the values inherently instilled in us through living that kind of life. Not that "city folk" don't have values, but all we ever heard about those areas on the news was rampant crime. On the other hand, it was an unusually big deal when the "TV people" ever came to our small town. We were a community that helped one another out when the need arose, and we were able to provide that help because we understood the value of knowing how to do things ourselves. We didn't call someone else in to do our jobs for us and were always ready and willing to extend a helping hand to our neighbors when they needed it. That innate comfort in working hard and helping others is something I've always carried with me.

Fast-forward to heading off to college. In spectacular average-Joe fashion, I had no idea what I wanted to do with my life. I only knew that I was supposed to go to college, get a job, work hard, and then retire. So when I got to Longwood University (though back then it was a college) and they asked me to pick a major, I looked at their list, saw physics, and figured because I'd taken one physics class in high school and passed it, that was the right path for me. And I actually managed to stick it out all the way through graduation and get a physics degree with a concentration in engineering as well as a math minor. I even enjoyed it on occasion.

But the real impact my time in college had on me actually had nothing to do with college at all. Instead, it had everything to do with a buddy of mine knowing exactly the right words to say to a kid with a college-age mentality.

When he first tried to convince me that we should become volunteer firefighters for the local station, I was less than enthusiastic. I admittedly wasn't even aware that volunteer firefighters *existed*, let alone understood why anyone would willingly put themselves up to a job like that with no pay. But then he said the magic words: "They have a pool table at the station."

And the rest, as they say, is history.

Playing pool was a nice perk, but I truly fell in love with being a firefighter. Sure, it was challenging and time consuming, far from a "part-time" or "volunteer" schedule. But that was part of what kept me coming back. The work was so engaging and rewarding that I couldn't help but put in 110 percent effort, even as a volunteer. I wasn't able to perform EMT duties (at least, not yet), but I regularly responded to fires, car accidents, gas leaks, and other emergencies. I earned Volunteer Firefighter of the Year, and my buddy and I consistently remained in the top-five bracket of responders year over year. I loved being part of something bigger than myself and having the opportunity to truly help people in their greatest times of need. I knew it was something I would continue to do for a long time.

The only problem was that volunteer work didn't pay the bills. So after I graduated college with my physics degree, I decided to put it to use by working as an engineer for a local truss company. We designed and manufactured roof and floor trusses for residential building components, and that too, was satisfying work in its own way. It felt good to actually use my college education to earn money. But I'd be lying if I said I wasn't looking forward to the day when I would actually make money working as a firefighter.

About two years later, that day finally came. There's a lot of joy in finally getting paid to do what you love, and I even got my EMT cardiac technician (EMT-CT) certification when the new department hired me. I finally felt like a full-fledged career firefighter, and that was exhilarating. Of course, what they *don't* tell you amid all that joy is that a fresh firefighter's salary is anything but glamorous. If you're a first responder or frontline worker like me, I probably don't need to tell you that twice.

But I was in it for the long haul. Firefighting was my career. I wasn't going anywhere, and I saw the potential upward mobility of being a firefighter. So I found a way to juggle things part time with the truss company and full time with the fire department. And it worked well enough. I was able to support my wife and our young daughter, though my wife will always say my obsession with firefighting is an illness. "Who in their right mind runs into a building on fire while everyone else is running out?" she used to ask. To which I would respond, "Who ever said I was in my right mind?"

A handful of years went by that way, until the Great Recession hit our country at the end of 2007. People stopped construction on homes and commercial buildings, which meant I got laid off from the truss company. And though I still had the firefighting job I loved, I had never worked only one job at a time in my life. In a way, I felt unemployed, and I needed more to do. I've never been one to just sit around if I have enough bandwidth to get stuff done. So when I was watching HGTV one day and saw a home inspector checking out properties to determine the integrity of the build, I figured I could do that job. People weren't building homes, but some were still buying them, which meant there was still a need for home inspectors. I'd always been interested in construction and had a closely related background, so why not do home inspections around my firefighting schedule to fill in the gaps? To that end, I called up a local home-inspection company (which was just a single-man operation), asked for a job, got my inspector certification, and started with him part time.

Fast-forward a couple years. I decided to branch out and start my own home-inspection business. Today, Clatterbuck Home Inspections employs a handful of people, who provide hundreds of certified home inspections each year. I run a steady and successful business that I'm proud of, but it's certainly been a hefty learning process to get to this point. When I started, I wasn't educated in how to form or run a business. I really had no idea what I was doing except for the inspection part of things. But based on my previous position working for someone else, I did recognize there were processes and operations that could be better, so I set out to make that a reality. Little did I know that kind of can-do, action-focused mindset (and maybe a little bit of blind faith) would serve me well in starting to invest in real estate too.

But this isn't a home-inspection book. It's not even a firefighting book. It's a book about real estate investing. And though those other two industries play a huge role in who I am and how I conduct my business, they are not the reason I can call myself "the millionaire fire-fighter." That, again, has to do with someone saying the right words to me at the right time.

I was out on an inspection one day, and the buyer of the home mentioned he was planning to rent the property out to tenants. Purely for conversational purposes, I asked how much he'd be charging in rent, and when he told me, my jaw nearly hit the floor. One piece of information a home inspector is privy to is the purchase price of the house they're inspecting, so when I did the math and compared that amount to the rent he'd be charging (which was very reasonable for the time and location), I realized he would be making a nice sum of money. But it went a step further than that. It dawned on me that this guy had to be some kind of genius, because in less than thirty years, he was going to own a home that someone else had paid for—and then some.

It struck me then and there that this was a concept I'd be dumb not to explore further. I didn't know anything about buying real estate for rental purposes, but I had to find out if it was an option for someone like me. At that time, I was working upward of sixty hours a week, making only $60,000 per year, and I didn't have much in the way of savings or assets. Not to mention, I was the only one providing income for my household. Was I crazy to even consider this as a possibility?

As luck would have it—though many people feel very differently about that time in history—this was all unfolding in 2009, after the housing crash of 2008. That means homes were going for cheaper than they normally would. I found a townhome in my area available for short sale (more on what that means later) and looked at my purchasing options. To be honest, there weren't many for me to consider. But by that point, I was determined. I was going to find a way to make it work, no matter what it took.

Through diligent research, I came across an option called a home equity line of credit (HELOC). We were fortunate to own (with a mortgage) the house we lived in, so we took out a HELOC on it and used that line of credit as the down payment we otherwise didn't have for the townhome. For some perspective, the down payment and closing costs were about $16,000 on a property costing $135,000. These numbers may seem small by today's standards, but for us back then, it was a *lot* of money. Even with the HELOC, my wife and I were putting a lot of money down relative to our household income. It took some hefty convincing for her to finally agree to let me go through with it. And once I applied, the couple months it took for everything to be approved were some of the most nerve-racking months of my life.

But in the end, I did it. My not-so-harebrained scheme had worked, and I officially had my first rental property. I fixed it up and got tenants into it, and they started paying off my mortgage for me. Any extra cash I earned from their rent payments went right back into managing and maintaining the property, so I wasn't making much of anything on that first rental, but it didn't matter. What kept me going was that I had already realized the most incredible and valuable part of this whole process: In thirty years, I'd own a house that someone else had paid for.

Just like I had become hooked on being a fire-fighter, I became hooked on investing in real estate. And just like it had been a nerve-racking experience to start my own home-inspection business, it was incredibly nerve-racking to figure out how to purchase my first rental property. But by exploring my options, being open to creative solutions, and taking the first leap, I made it happen. And two years later, after learning valuable insights from the first property, I bought a second investment property right across the street. Then I bought a third property that same year. And those numbers have only gone up from there.

Today, I own about twenty single-family and multi-family rental units in North Carolina and South Carolina. Yes, I still reside in the same area where I grew up in Virginia. It might surprise you to learn that I don't own rental property where I live, but the reason behind that is deliberately calculated and also something I'll cover a little later.

In hindsight, had I known during my first purchase what I now know about investing, such as how the market changes and everything in between, I would have found a way to purchase a dozen homes back in 2009. In fact, I will always say that the best time to buy an investment property was twenty years ago, and the next-best time to buy is today.

At the same time, I have no regrets about any of the decisions I've made up to this point. Not about how I grew up, what I did in college, the career path I chose, or the financial decisions I made. I don't regret any of it; every single decision has led me to where I am today. And I'm happy with my self-taught and self-made success because it allows me to live the life I want. It also allows me to help others figure out how to live the lives they want.

So since we can't go back to 2009 and buy a bunch of properties, let's focus on right now and looking ahead to the future. If you want to affect change in your life through building wealth, then it's up to you to not only figure out how to go about it but to understand why *you* must be the one to figure it out. There are so many important factors that can (and should) influence the reasons behind choosing a path that leads to building more wealth. Let's explore some of them so that you better understand where you are and what knowledge you still need to gain in order to get yourself where you want to go.

CHAPTER TWO

YOU ARE YOUR BEST CHANCE AT WEALTH

I THINK IT'S PRETTY SAFE TO SAY that everyone wants more money. Except for possibly the multibillionaires of the world (and even they keep finding ways to further line their pockets), just about anyone will gladly take more money when the opportunity arises.

But there's a key word in that sentence that makes all the difference in achieving the true freedom that comes with more money: *take*.

People will gladly *take* money when it's presented to them. What people rarely do is *create* more money for themselves when the opportunity to do so exists. And that's the number-one problem holding many people back from building wealth. They rely on other people or the circumstances around them to financially get them by in life. They're complacent with the money offered to them by things like their employer or their pension plan, believing that if these systems and processes exist the way they do, then that's all there is to it, and life is meant to go on just that way forever and always.

This mindset is largely due to most people just failing to grasp—or maybe deliberately avoiding—the concept that there are so many ways to create more wealth for themselves outside of the job they work. Many people just assign themselves to a life of accepting what's laid out plainly in front of them instead of finding ways to actively earn more wealth. Maybe they assume it's too difficult or that it requires a higher education or that someone will eventually just do it for them. And because of that, their finances and their life will remain as they have always been. And I'm no exception to this mindset—sometimes it's nice to just coast through parts of life. But that mindset has to be temporary.

HANDOUTS DON'T LEAD TO WEALTH

Except for maybe trust-fund babies or beneficiaries of generational wealth, no one gets ahead by exclusively relying on happenstance handouts they receive throughout their lifetime. And this is even true when it might seem like others are actually attempting to help you get ahead when it comes to money.

The example I like to use to best illustrate this point is our United States government. There have been many times throughout our history, and even very recently, when it seems like they are coming to our rescue in times of financial crisis or need. For example, during the COVID-19 pandemic, they handed out stimulus checks. And of course, people gladly took them. It was free money, after all.

But how quickly did that money disappear? How many people do you think either still have that money sitting in a rainy-day fund or decided to invest it and turn it into more money? If I were a betting man, I'd put my money on "not many." And that's because most people *needed* to spend that money in order to help themselves or their families survive. And therein lies the problem with handouts of that sort: It's always enough money to get by, and never enough to get ahead. Free money even creates inflation; there's too much capital chasing too few goods.

The same goes for things like pension programs or Social Security. Yes, you're contributing to those funds on the front end while you work, but the government sure is doing something nice by setting up a system to provide money to you after you retire, right? Well, not exactly. If you look at what those plans and funds *actually* provide on a monthly basis, you'll see that the money likely won't give you the means to live the life you truly want. It's why so many people end up having to take second jobs after retirement. I'm not knocking Social

Security by any means, but it doesn't provide for an adequate retirement. The same goes for 401(k) and 457 retirement plans. You contribute pretax funds to those, which lowers your taxable income, and that's great. But you pay the taxes on them when you withdraw, and that will be at a higher rate than when you contributed since, with few exceptions, taxes are always higher in the future than they are today. So these plans tend to just not be enough to comfortably rely on in retirement.

The point I'm making with all this relates back to determining what "being wealthy" means to you. If being wealthy involves anything beyond what the salary you're earning or the handouts you're receiving can provide you with, then the truth is simple: You cannot rely on that money alone to get you there. If you envision a different life for yourself, one that includes the financial freedom to live the way you want, you can only rely on yourself to supply the funds to make that happen. I don't care how many checks the government gives you; *you* are your own best chance at building wealth. Not them and not anyone else.

This concept might seem so obvious that it's not worth dissecting, and I really wish that were true. However, throughout my life, I've seen so much evidence that points to the contrary that it truly feels worth examining before diving into the specifics of how real estate can help you achieve a higher level of building wealth.

FIND THE THINGS WORTH FIGHTING FOR

There are so many admirable causes to fight for in life, and a lot of those causes benefit not only you and your life but also possibly the lives of those around you. A great example is my firefighting career.

As a firefighter, I'm part of a union by choice. And every few years, several members of our union demand an increase in salary. I'm always supportive of it, as it is, of course, entirely justified. The work we do merits higher pay and better benefits because we're putting our lives and well-being on the line for others every day, and that hard work deserves to be recognized and rewarded. The union often fights for an annual 3 percent salary increase, but a lot of years we fight for more, because we actually got less than 3 percent the previous year.

So much time and effort goes into these salary-increase requests, with negotiations sometimes spanning the better part of a year. And when they're successful at 3 percent (or less), it only results in a few thousand dollars of additional earnings added to our yearly salary. And while I'm incredibly appreciative of that increase, I always find myself thinking that getting there took a lot of energy and time, especially when you think about its impact on the grand scheme of things. Why not instead expend that energy on something that can *really* make a difference to your finances and well-being? Or at the very least, after you're done fighting for an increased salary, why not carry that momentum into other ventures that can do great things for you while your mentality is in exactly the right place for it?

Fighting for 3 percent year after year isn't going to change your life, but educating yourself about what else is out there, exploring investment opportunities, and taking action like starting your own business . . . *that* can change your life. And like I've already said, doing so doesn't have to mean giving up everything you love. My ongoing career as a firefighter is living proof of that.

But it does mean being willing to put some work into understanding where you are, what you want, and the best ways to get there. It means taking your financial education and endeavors into your own hands. No one is going to provide those things for you. You *must* seek them out on your own if you want to reap the rewards that come with them.

LINING UP THE STEPS

To start, you need to ask yourself what "being wealthy" looks like to you. You need to set a goal that clearly dictates what point you're trying to reach. It can be a number in your bank account. It can be the ability to purchase the luxury items you've always wanted. It can be achieving peace of mind when it comes to your finances, meaning you don't lose sleep wondering if you'll be able to pay all your bills next month. Identify exactly what "wealth" looks like to you, and let it motivate you on this journey. Your picture of wealth may change along the way, and that's okay. Life is full of change, but that's what keeps us moving forward. As long as you readjust alongside any such changes so that you can keep a clear picture of your own wealth in your mind, you'll be in good shape.

The next step after defining what wealth looks like for you is to provide yourself with an education in all the ways you can achieve it. And notice how I said "provide yourself." Again, no one is going to give that to you. Yes, there are books, coaches, classes, and more available from other people out there, but no one is going to force you to sit down and take them in. The choice to take advantage of what they have to offer is entirely up to you.

In the case of building wealth, your education is going to be actively exploring all the options available to you for building that wealth. If you're reading this book, you might be tempted to skip this step because you've already decided that real estate is the option you'll be utilizing, but I actually encourage you to explore and research *all* the options available out there. Understand how things like stocks, bonds, and cryptocurrencies work. Determine if any of these other options might make sense for you. The best thing that can happen is you discover something that really intrigues you and can work well for your situation. The worst thing that can happen is you eliminate anything that doesn't resonate with you and you're left with the option that makes the most sense, giving you a clearer path ahead.

Really take the time to listen to different perspectives from different types of people who are experts with these investment options and engage in learning from them. Listen to what they're doing to build wealth and see what understanding you reap from it. You may even discover that having multiple types of investments works well for you. Personally, I have investments in stocks and cryptocurrency in addition to real estate. Sure, real estate is 90 percent of my portfolio, but I like having just a little bit of diversification. And though I'm not an expert in stocks or crypto the same way I am in real estate, I've learned a lot about those alternative options from real experts in each respective industry.

Only when you gain an understanding of something can you better decide how to utilize it in your own life. And the best way to gain that understanding is by learning from others. That's why I always say that if you're the smartest person in the room, you're in the wrong room.

However, you should never do what people say just because they're telling you to do it. And that goes for me too! This is where the self-education factor is so key. Exploring your options and listening to the words shared by experts is important, but the other critical part is deciding for yourself how you will (or won't) use the information provided. As an example, I've always tried to learn from the officers I've worked alongside in the fire service. From some of them, I've learned positive traits like how to be a better leader; from others, I've learn what not to do. But either way, I learned. And you can only gain that kind of insight if you also educate yourself about exactly what it is you're looking for, where you currently stand, and why you're ready to take the next steps. I call that process "figuring out your Why," and Chapter 4 of this book details how to go about doing just that.

For now, you may actually find yourself at a bit of a crossroads. I've encouraged you to self-educate and take things into your own hands by exploring your options, learning from experts, and determining what options will work best for you because only by fully relying on and committing to yourself can you start down the road to achieving wealth. But it's up to you to make the all-important choice of how you'll go about doing it.

If you've done the research and reflective thinking and have still decided that investing in real estate is your best option forward, then I'm thrilled to hear that's the case. That means you're ready to dive a little deeper into how those processes work and what they might look like for you.

It's time to learn the ins and outs of why real estate is such a great choice for building wealth so that you're equipped with the knowledge you'll need as you get started.

CHAPTER THREE

WHAT MAKES REAL ESTATE A GREAT INVESTMENT

I WILL ALWAYS BE THE FIRST PERSON to say that anyone can invest in real estate. That's absolutely true. But I will also be the first person to admit there's a lot to learn about real estate before investing in it. Like any other industry, real estate has its own laws, concepts, terms, jargon, and more that you need to be at least somewhat familiar with if you want to understand your options and how to take advantage of them.

So that's what this chapter aims to do. It won't be an exhaustive breakdown of every single term or nuance in real estate (again, there are tons of excellent books out there for a deep dive further into those elements). But it will give you a comprehensive overview of what makes real estate such a great investment choice, as well as explain a few critical elements and concepts every savvy investor needs to know.

At the back of this book, you'll also find an index of real estate–related terminology that should be helpful for understanding some of the jargon this book and other resources will likely reference. Though I'll explain some terms along the way, feel free to flip ahead to that alphabetical list for reference as needed while you read.

WHAT IS "INVESTING"?

To start, let's talk about what "investing in real estate" actually means. In terms of this book and the industry I'm referring to, I like to define "investing" as "owning real estate for both the current and future financial benefit of it."

You might think purchasing a home to live in has both current and future benefits, but the reality is that your primary residence doesn't really benefit you financially. It's still a liability you have to pay for out of your own pocket month after month, and it will only benefit you financially in the future if you sell it and its value has risen (that's called "appreciation"). But even then, if you're selling your house and plan to purchase a new one to live in, then all the money you make on the sale—or at least a large portion of it—is just going to go right back into purchasing that new primary residence. That doesn't make for a great way to help you build your wealth. As said many times by the great Robert Kiyosaki, "Assets put money in your pocket; liabilities take money out of your pocket."

So investing in real estate means you're investing in a *non*-primary residence with the intention of benefiting yourself financially with it now or later or sometimes both. If your goal is to generate money from it now, you can rent it out to tenants and charge them enough in rent to cover your monthly mortgage payments and other property necessities as well as to provide some additional cash. If you're looking to benefit down the road, you do the same thing, but you continuously put those additional earnings back into improving the property or into purchasing more properties so that when the time comes to sell, you have more and better assets that will gain you larger payouts.

Granted, those are two very basic breakdowns of how, generally, real estate investing can work. The reality is that there are all *kinds* of ways to make investments, with all types of properties, deals, arrangements, and more. But for the sake of this book and understanding the basics, when I talk about investing in real estate, I'm talking about purchasing properties like single-family homes, townhomes, and condos, or multifamily properties like apartments, duplexes, and fourplexes for the purpose of renting them to tenants for cash flow, property appreciation, and useful tax benefits.

But even then, real estate investing, whether purchasing, selling, or taking all the steps in between, is a little more nuanced than that. There are things about it you're going to want to understand, not only for the purpose of doing them yourself but for understanding *why* they should be done at all.

Let's start by considering what you want to use your real estate investments for. It comes back to cash flow and appreciation in value, and preferably both at the same time. When I first started out, I went into my first townhome purchase with the intention of focusing on the long-term equity (or value) of the property. So despite making some extra money every month from the rent I charged (even after covering additional expenses for the property like utilities, insurance, and general upkeep), I was putting all that money back into the property to make it better. That's because even though it would have been great to have that extra money in my pocket, I knew the more I increased the value of the home now, the more it would be worth later.

Let's say you buy a property to rent, and you earn additional cash flow (after the mortgage payment and expenses have been paid) of $300 per month on it. That means in five years you'll have made $18,000. But if you chose your property correctly, paid the right price for it, and took care of it by putting that cash back into it over the last five years, it could have the potential to appreciate in value to $50,000 (or more) in those five years. Knowing that potential number, that $18,000 doesn't feel quite as exciting, does it? But again, it's all about deciding what you want out of your investment: extra cash flow now, more value later, or a way to make a little bit of each work. My personal aim is to always go for the last option.

Any way you work it, appreciation of the property is the key here, and it's going to be your best friend. So let's break down how it works.

UNDERSTANDING APPRECIATION

Real estate is such a fantastic investment choice because there's almost a guarantee (*almost*) of it increasing in value over time. That's because there will always be a need for housing. This inherent human necessity will never go away, so there will always be people looking to rent homes, townhomes, and apartments who otherwise have no desire or discipline to purchase a house for themselves. And if you combine that need with the steadily increasing costs of living and the increasing market prices of homes to reflect those costs, you have a recipe for reliable appreciation of your home's value.

When you invest in real estate, you invest in something that's almost certain to have more value down the road. You can't always say that for stocks or cryptocurrency. I guarantee that if you walked into a bank and asked them for a $50,000 loan to put into stock purchases, they would turn you down. But if you did the same thing in order to purchase a house, they would most likely agree to it (depending on some other qualifying factors like your credit score, debt-to-income ratio, and job stability). That's because they see the long-term value and safety in purchasing real estate.

And though the value of your property later most heavily depends on the general housing market at any given time, it also relies on a lot of elements that you can directly control, such as where you've decided to purchase and any improvements you've made to the property.

Even so, gaining meaningful appreciation on a property takes time. I always tell people that real estate investing is by no means a get-rich-quick scheme. It takes patience and willingness to hold on to a property for five, ten, twenty, and sometimes thirty years before it makes sense to cash in on its increased value.

For that reason, think of real estate investing like planting a forest: If your goal is to create a thick, lush, self-sustaining forest, all you can do is plant one tree at a time and then wait for each tree to grow. You can't rush the process, and you can't rely on just a single tree to make up the entire forest you're aiming for. That's not how forests work. To create a forest, you need more and more trees, and the patience to both plant and watch those trees grow.

The same goes for real estate investing. If you want seamless and ongoing cash flow and/or reliable value increase that you can count on later in life, you have to consider making multiple investments that you're willing to hold on to for long periods of time. But another awesome thing about real estate investing is that it comes with some incredible rules and laws that help to make both of these things achievable.

REFINANCING AND REINVESTING

Let's go back to that example of $50,000 worth of appreciation on a property over the course of five years. It was your very first investment property, and you've been eager to purchase another but have no idea how you can possibly scrounge together the money for another investment while *also* holding on to your first investment to continue letting it appreciate. In other words, you're wondering how you're supposed to pay for all the trees in this forest you're trying to plant.

Luckily for you, it's almost like the real estate system is built specifically to help with exactly that. If you've been smart about purchasing your first property, putting the work and care into it that it needs, and letting it appreciate, you have likely created "usable equity" in your property, which means a total value that exceeds your outstanding mortgage balance. You can take advantage of that equity through something called a "cash-out refinance."

A cash-out refinance is a type of loan taken out on a piece of property you already own. Essentially, it's a new home loan for more than what you currently owe on your property because the value of the home has increased since you purchased it. The monetary difference between that new mortgage amount and the balance on your previous mortgage is paid out to you in cash, and you can use it however you'd like. In other words, if your home has appreciated by $50,000 over the last five years, through a cash-out refinance you now have $50,000 to spend on a down payment for your next investment property. You can basically purchase another property *for free* because the money you're putting down on the house isn't coming out of your own pocket—it's coming directly from your lender by way of refinancing.

But do you know what the very best part of this strategy is? This type of transaction is completely tax-free because, whereas when you normally sell a property, you have to pay taxes on that sale because of your earnings from it, in a cash-out refinance, you're technically borrowing the money from your lender and are expected to pay it back in increments over time. So the IRS does not consider that cash as taxable income to you—even though you're going to use it to supplement your income over the long run.

This is the beauty of real estate investing. The system is set up to help you succeed in using it to generate wealth.

THE FOUR WAYS TO MAKE MONEY IN REAL ESTATE

There are at least four reliable and proven ways to make money in real estate. The first is the cash flow you receive every month from rent. That entails the difference between the rental income you're making versus all your expenses for owning and running the property. Whatever's left over is yours to keep and do with what you'd like.

The second is paying down the principal of your mortgage. Every month when you make your mortgage payment to your lender—or really, when your tenant pays your mortgage via the rent you're charging them—part of that payment goes to the principal (the loan amount itself), and part of it goes to the interest (the additional rate the lender is charging you on top of your loan for borrowing that money). When it comes to interest payments, you actually get to write that off on your taxes every year. So the principal is equity that you're generating from your property every year. And at the end of your mortgage, that principal will have been paid down to zero. But even as the principal is being paid and goes away, the house is generating equity through appreciation.

The third way is actually through depreciation—or your property losing value over time. This might sound confusing considering I've just detailed how appreciation is the name of the game. But there's a bit of an interesting tax law that Congress wrote specifically pertaining to this that's very much worth taking advantage of if you own investment properties. In general, the overall value of a piece of property tends to increase over time thanks to market and housing demands. However, the materials and components that make up the house or apartment—the wood, the bricks, the mortar—are getting older and older each year, making them less and less valuable over time. Well, there are ways to calculate that specific type of depreciation of those building materials and report its value as a loss on your taxes. That means you can actually report to the IRS that you lost money on a particular piece of real estate even if the property didn't actually cost you any money. This in turn lowers your tax burden on your property. The most seasoned real estate investors know that, if you're doing things right, at the end of each fiscal year, you should really never owe any taxes on your real estate properties. If you're doing real estate right, you're losing money on paper but not in your bank account!

The fourth and final way to make money through real estate investing is the straight appreciation of your property. You own an asset (the property) that is continually increasing in value. What's great is that even though the value of the asset you own is increasing, the money you owe on it is not (as long as you have a fixed mortgage, meaning your interest rate doesn't fluctuate). In other words, over time, as our economy experiences inflation, you'll still be paying the same amount for your mortgage every single month as your property value increases. So twenty years down the road, that $1,000 per month you've always been paying is, thanks to the economy and your appreciation, going to be smaller in comparison to the value of the property at that future point in time. So you're paying with "cheaper dollars" in the future because the value of a dollar decreases year over year. This is why real estate is such a good deal: because of the debt.

DEBT IS A GOOD THING

Yes, you read that right. When it comes to real estate, being in debt is a good thing. And that's such an important fact to know and thoroughly understand about investing. So let go of all the negative notions and misconceptions you might have about debt always being the villain and how you need to avoid it at all costs. When it comes to real estate, debt is not the enemy.

For people who don't understand debt or know how to manage it, fear is the natural reaction to it and avoiding taking any on is understandable. But to get over those fears, you have to understand the difference between good debt and bad debt. And you can break that down by understanding an "asset" versus a "liability": Assets are good, while liabilities are bad.

Simply put, an asset is something that puts money in your pocket. A liability is something that takes money out of your pocket. So if you have credit card debt, that's a liability, or bad debt, because it's money you owe on purchases with no hope of spinning what you owe into earnings for yourself. If you finance a car, that's also bad debt because you're paying money out of your pocket to pay it off, and on top of that, the car is decreasing in value every month you keep it. There's nothing to be gained there.

Rental properties, on the other hand, are an asset, or good debt. When you take out a mortgage on a property, you owe money to your lender, which creates debt for yourself. But if you're renting the property for more than you owe on that mortgage every month, your debt is actually putting money in your pocket. Your mortgage is covered, *and* you're earning additional money.

Keep in mind that if you own the home you live in, that's actually not an asset. That's a liability. Your primary residence is not putting money into your pocket the same way a tenant in a rental unit would be. You're paying your personal mortgage out of your own pocket every single month. Your primary residence's mortgage is taking money away from you without replenishing it. Yes, your property will appreciate over time, but in the meantime, you have bad debt, or a liability, on your hands.

It's so important to understand that even though purchasing investment properties will give you debt, that debt is your friend. In fact, it's the thing that's going to help you build wealth. So don't run from it—embrace it. But make sure you thoroughly understand how it works first. You want the arbitrage of the debt: borrowing money and making a payment but ultimately receiving more than the payments you owe!

CHOOSING THE RIGHT PROPERTY

Earlier in this chapter, I mentioned choosing "your property correctly" as a critical part of building your wealth with real estate. While most properties tend to appreciate over time, there are always going to be "better" choices to make about where and what you purchase. Some of it has to do with your goals and means, while some of it has to do with the location of the property and the actual property itself.

I currently do not own any rental property in the city I live in. I don't even own rental property in the *state* I live in. And that's not because I don't love where I live. It's because I did the research that showed me that purchasing and renting out homes in my area was not the best fiscal choice for me in relation to my overarching goal, which is to build wealth as best I can.

Where I live, the cost of housing ownership has increased faster than the cost of rent has increased, so it was cost-prohibitive for me to continue purchasing properties here to then rent out, because the purchase-to-rent ratio wouldn't have worked in my favor. I eventually realized that it made much more sense to sell off the assets I had purchased where I live and to then use that equity to purchase different assets elsewhere. In North Carolina and South Carolina where I currently own rental property, I was able to purchase two houses for every one house I sold in Virginia.

Choosing the right property comes down to understanding what you want most out of this investing process and what kind of work you're willing to put into that process. And then there are so many additional factors to consider. I'll go into some of those additional factors in a later chapter, but for now, understand that being successful with real estate investing doesn't mean just choosing any random available property within your budget and hitting go. It requires researching various markets, understanding all the points of value a potential property has (or lacks), comparing those elements with the goals you have for this process and the way you want to manage your business, then seeing how you can make all the puzzle pieces fit together in the most beneficial way.

COMMON MISCONCEPTIONS ABOUT RENTAL PROPERTIES

Understanding how the game of real estate works and how it can be so beneficial for building wealth is the first important step. But even after many people have wrapped their brains around those concepts, they still have concerns about diving in. Over the years, I've found that a majority of those lingering concerns are due to the many myths and misconceptions people hear about owning and managing rental properties, so I want to debunk some of the most common ones.

The first misconception is that tenants can't be trusted and will just destroy your property. People considering buying homes or apartments to rent have a fear that whoever they put in the living space is just going to trash it, and they're going to lose all the value in their property or have to pour thousands and thousands of dollars into repairs. Now, I won't lie and say that's impossible, because of course it's possible. But the reality is that you're going to put safeguards in place to minimize losses. Having a good property manager, whether it's you or someone else, means having someone who knows how to screen tenants properly. The beauty of owning your own property is that you get to decide who you rent it out to. So if you do your due diligence, you'll end up with good, reliable tenants who you don't need to worry about. Property management is the key to successfully owning and operating rental property.

For catastrophic events such as severe weather, fires, floods, etc., you will have property insurance in place as an added layer of protection. That's a requirement, and if you choose good insurance, you'll have good coverage and you won't break the bank making any necessary repairs. With this in hand, it's extremely unlikely that you'll lose all value in your property.

The second misconception people have is one I've already touched on: that to own all these properties, you have to maintain and manage them all yourself, day and night, no matter what might be occurring. I understand the dread in that, because no one wants to get a phone call at three o'clock in the morning asking them to fix an overflowing toilet—myself included. But you know what? I don't receive those phone calls. Ever. That's because I've hired excellent property managers to take care of all those processes for me.

Just because you own a rental property does not mean you have to be in charge of managing it. Though you certainly can do that job yourself if you'd like. I did it for the first ten years I owned property because I really wanted to learn the ins and outs of running things, and quite frankly, was too cheap to pay someone when I only lived ten minutes away. And doing so prepared me to hire the right property manager to take over from there.

Now, those experts do everything managerial for me, like interviewing new tenants, getting their leases signed, collecting rent, managing the upkeep and maintenance of properties, being on call when emergencies happen, and just about everything else you can think of. They make it so I can reap all the rewards of owning a rental property without having to worry about the nitty-gritty details that come with it. It makes things so much more hands-off and less stressful. Yes, these managers do require a fee, and it generally tends to be around 10 percent of rent. But you know what? That's easy money to part with in exchange for peace of mind that things are being taken care of without me having to put my thumb on top of every single detail of every single property. And you have the power to manage and maintain your properties and your tenants in the exact same way. Additionally, a professional property manager will pay for themselves by knowing the market rent, when to raise rent, how to evict tenants, and just good overall management skills!

The final misconception I want to touch on is the idea that you could never possibly have enough money to buy your first property. Sure, there's no denying that homes have gotten more and more expensive over the decades. That's how real estate works (which you've now learned is actually to our advantage as property owners). But going in hand with these increases are assistance programs to help with down payments and interest rates. If you're a first-time homebuyer or part of other designated groups of the population (such as military veterans), there are so many options available that make your loan processes easier.

If you're not a first-time homebuyer and currently own the home you live in, then there are so many ways to leverage the property you have in order to help with your next purchase. And if you don't fit into any of these categories, there are always ways to go about saving up the money you need for a down payment. I'll cover these concepts in more detail in the next chapter, but in the meantime, don't let the myth that "not everyone can buy a house" keep you from making this dream a reality. It's possible, no matter where you currently find yourself.

IT'S STILL A BUSINESS

The last thing that's absolutely crucial to understand about investing in real estate is this: Even though it's intended to be an additional form of income on top of doing the job you already have and love, it should still be treated like its own business.

Though owning real estate is a form of passive income, there are still certain things about it that need to be set up and managed properly if you want to ensure that it can *continue* to be a passive form of income with as little headache as possible. For example, you should set up an LLC for your properties (I'll dive into why in a later chapter), create a separate bank account for all its related business dealings, and approach running things with a business mindset. All your properties should have proper insurance coverage, and you should keep all those necessary documents organized and accessible. The same goes for any property managers you hire. Though they'll be doing the bulk of the legwork, you still have to manage the managers. They'll still turn to you with questions and needs, and you, as the business owner, have to be ready to provide them.

You don't need a business degree to be a successful real estate investor. I certainly don't have one. But what I *do* have is years of experience filled with taking time to learn all about what it takes to run this kind of business and the subsequent experience to put that knowledge to the test. The same knowledge I discovered in that way is available out there to you too.

Don't disregard the knowledge that's out there, but also don't get distracted by it. There's a right time and place to fill your head with all the exciting know-how available at your fingertips, and this chapter has only touched on some of that valuable knowledge. But before you go exploring all that information further, there's something much more important to focus on: yourself.

Before even starting this process, you have to have as much knowledge as possible about yourself and what you want. Knowing and understanding where you stand, what you want to achieve, and how you're going to get there is the single most important step you will take on this journey. Because without that personal insight, your fire for investment will have no kindling to keep it going in the long run.

CHAPTER FOUR
SETTING YOURSELF UP FOR SUCCESS

BEFORE YOU CAN EVEN HOP ON ZILLOW to start saving all the properties you're interested in or plan all the updates you're going to make to a property or envision the tenants you're going to interview and how you're going to invest your extra cash flow, you have to understand why you want to do all those things and how to make them possible.

Without a clear sense of not only which way you want to move but how you're going to propel yourself in that specific direction, you make it that much harder to actually get there. You can't start without knowing where you stand or where you're trying to end up.

Figuring out your reason for taking this endeavor on and for making the sacrifices you're going to make is going to be the thing that fuels your fire to keep going.

From there, figuring out how you're going to go about actually getting it done will be your road map to that destination.

START WITH YOUR "WHY"

It's all good and well to say, "I want to own a rental property." But if you were making small talk about it at a party and a stranger asked you, "Why do you want to own a rental property?" do you know what you would tell them? The obvious answer might be, "To make more money." But let's say this stranger really wanted to get to know you, so they asked, "Why do you want to make more money?" *Then* what would you say?

That's where your Why comes in. What is it that you truly want to get out of this process? Do you need a little extra cash flow every month so that you're not feeling the stress of living paycheck to paycheck? Are you trying to generate savings to put into a college fund for your kids? Are you trying to create more wealth now so that you can supplement your retirement later?

My own Why is for the long-term benefits. Yes, the cash flow does help me to have some reserves to rely on now so that I don't have to be stressed about paying bills, covering emergencies, or planning vacations when I want to take them. But I got into this thing, first and foremost, with my eyes set on the future. I want to own a piece of property (or multiple pieces of property) down the line that someone else paid for and gain the benefits of that fact when that time comes. I want to be comfortable in my retirement without having to worry when I'm already on the other side of it, because I'll have already worried about it well before. Then I can be completely free and comfortable to do all the other things I want to fill my days with.

In order to find success with investing in real estate, you have to stop defining your motivation in broad or vague terms. This is the time to really narrow your focus and find the inspiration behind your decision to take this endeavor on. There's no wrong answer except to not have one at all. So get to the root of your Why and let it motivate you through this process. It's ultimately going to be the thing that determines all the factors surrounding the how, where, and what behind your decision to invest. Don't lose sight of it, or you'll lose sight of the way through to your goal.

GET YOUR FINANCIAL HOUSE IN ORDER

When it all comes down to it, this is about money. It's about figuring out how to generate more wealth (for a specific purpose, of course) using the means you currently have or the means you can create. So a large part of this process must be getting your finances in order. And that has to happen before you even start. Because, again, if you don't know what you're working with, you can't know what you're capable of.

Spend a weekend sifting through every single one of your financial details. Look at your bank accounts—checking, savings, retirement funds, and any others—to gain an understanding of what your assets look like. Then look at your credit card statements and get a feel for how much you're spending every month and what you're spending on. Look at any recurring payments outside your credit card bills, such as your rent, utilities, car payments, and health insurance. Compare it all to your income to understand what your financial house currently looks like. When you have those numbers, you give yourself the ability to see what more you need to do or what you might need to change in order to make real estate investing a better possibility. For absolute clarity on where you stand, you can even put together a profit and loss statement (P and L) and a personal financial statement (PFS) for your current situation.

Once you really understand all your finances, you may discover that you do have the means to make that first rental property a reality, then you can go for it. Or you might reveal ways that you need to start saving some extra cash for that purpose, and you can then start pouring your energy into tackling that next. Or you might discover other areas where you need to make adjustment, like if your credit score isn't in the best place.

That could mean using a credit-consulting firm to help raise your credit score before doing anything else.

Any way it goes, you can't start investing without having your finances in line. If the money isn't ready, then you aren't ready. You *must* have the financial means to handle all the things that are going to come up in relation to owning a rental property—and that doesn't just mean scrounging together the initial down payment to purchase a property. It means having the finances to make any necessary repairs or replacements to make the place desirable to live in. It means having some money to put into advertising that you have a place available for rent. It means having the money to pay a property manager if you don't want to handle the dirty work yourself. It means having the money for emergencies or unexpected occurrences that will inevitably pop up.

Get your financial house in order before you try to get an actual house in order. It will make the process much easier and much less stressful or burdensome.

DO THE RESEARCH

Similar to figuring out your Why is figuring out your What. What that means in this case is figuring out what kind of property you want to invest in and where you want that property to be, as well as understanding all the factors that go into making that decision and what can actually result from making it. In other words, the property you choose is a big deal, not just an afterthought.

Again, you can simply say, "I want to invest in real estate," but that can really mean anything and everything. If you don't narrow down where you want to make your investment and what kind of property you want to invest in, you'll likely become overwhelmed by all the options available—there are hundreds of thousands of properties available at any one time. But if you narrow your focus and set yourself some precise parameters for what exactly you're looking for, you'll make things that much easier for yourself.

As I mentioned earlier in this book, I no longer own any rental property in the state I live in. That's because after a few years of gaining experience, I finally gathered the knowledge I needed to realize that it made sense to start exploring other markets. And the decision to change the very core of where I do my business was actually a really easy one to make when I finally understood how much more money I could earn by doing so.

The great thing about reading this book now, at the beginning of your interest in learning more, is that you don't need to spend all the years I did learning that same lesson. I'm giving you that valuable knowledge right here, right now. The core of it is to put ample time and effort into learning what kind of property makes the most sense for what you want to achieve and how you want to operate things.

If you're a type A personality that needs to see and control your rental properties every single day in order to have the reassurance that things are running the way they should, you're going to want to find something available close to where you live. If you're more like me and don't mind hiring out a property manager to worry about those things for you and, as a result, are comfortable with almost *never* seeing or visiting the properties you purchase, the world is your oyster, and you can explore markets in any state. And if you might be somewhere in between and don't mind your property being out of town so long as you can check on it as needed, your scope of properties to explore will be a little scaled down from "countrywide" but a little more scaled up from "my backyard." It all depends on how you want to run things.

From there, you must decide what type of property you want to invest in. While there are other options available, the simplest place to start and where most first-time investors start, is with either single-family housing or small multifamily housing. A single-family home is a freestanding house or a townhouse or condo that's part of a larger building. Multifamily housing is something like a duplex (two separate units or dwellings in one building, and you own the entire building), a fourplex (the same as a duplex but with four units that you own), or even larger apartment complexes, which can range up to hundreds of units. But those tend to be much larger-scale investments that you likely won't be taking on for your first rodeo—though there's no stopping you if you decide that's the best course of action for your situation and your goals.

There are pros and cons to both types of housing. The somewhat standard line of thinking is that the more units on a property, the more money to be earned. But it also means more work to do to manage and maintain those units, and often, more money to purchase them. So it just depends on what kind of trade-off you're looking for. Either way, if you don't do the research to understand the types of properties available and what purchasing them may mean, you won't be able to make a sound decision for your first investment.

And even when you've locked down what kind of property you'd like to invest in, there are dozens of additional factors that contribute to whether a property is a smart purchase. Things like the location of the property (Is it close to shops? Schools? Public transportation? Nature? Other desirable amenities?), the demographic of potential renters (Is the neighborhood safe? Can renters in the area afford how much you want to charge?), the condition of the property (How old is it? What, if any, updates have been made? What repairs will you have to pay for?), and the price (Does the price of the property make sense in relation to other properties available in the area? Is the price something you can afford?) should all be further determining factors in your decision. But you won't know how to make this decision unless you put the research into where and what you buy.

TREAT IT LIKE A BUSINESS

I once had a tenant that I really wanted to get out of my unit as quickly as I could because I was losing money on them. They didn't have the financial means to keep paying rent, but this was during the peak outbreak of the COVID-19 pandemic, so we couldn't just evict them. But for every month they were staying in my unit and not paying rent on time, the mortgage was still due. So I had to make the most practical business decision possible for how I was going to solve this problem.

I offered the tenant $400 to help them locate and move to a new housing situation. It was to help them with their moving costs, and I would pay it to them in full as long as they promised to be out of my unit by a certain date without causing any damage to my property. And it worked like a charm.

To be honest, I really didn't feel like being this person's friend and helping them out. That tenant cost me thousands of dollars in mortgage payments as well as the additional $400 to finally get them out, and I certainly wasn't happy about that. But I knew it was the right decision to make because it helped my business in the larger scope of things.

That's how you have to think of your own rental business. You have to be willing to make hard choices and sacrifices that you likely don't want to make for the greater good of your business's well-being. There are going to be tough business decisions to make that may go against your emotions or your gut reactions to things. But it's a mindset you have to be prepared to take on.

Part of that means knowing exactly what's better for your business in the long run, and that knowledge comes from knowing the data of your business. You have to be willing to take time to understand the numbers that make up your business and how to utilize them to better your business. I was able to look at how much money I was losing and would continue to lose if I didn't do something versus how much money I could start bringing in again by sacrificing a little more up front. When I did that, paying the tenant to leave just plain made the most sense. But I never would have known that if I didn't have precise data in front of me to consider.

Treating this like a business involves keeping good financial records; having a business bank account, checks, and credit cards ready to use *only* for your business; and understanding the tax implications of the properties you own. And these are all things you can certainly hire people to handle for you, but again, that's a decision that must be made with data already in mind so you can determine if hiring out help is something feasible or worth doing.

That mindset also means, as I touched on in an earlier chapter, setting things up to run like a business. Investing in real estate involves lots of money floating in and out of various accounts, often in large quantities. You don't want to mingle those finances and transactions with your personal finances, because that's a quick way to make a mess of things. It doesn't benefit you financially and can actually compromise the integrity of your personal life if you ever find yourself in financial woes, such as facing a lawsuit.

My recommendation is to form a limited liability company (LLC) through which you will do all your real estate business dealings. You can file this entity online with your state for a few hundred dollars, and then you can open an associated business checking account and business credit cards. Operating as an LLC will position your investments as legitimate business dealings while also keeping your personal assets safe from seizure if anything ever goes sideways. And the associated banking for that LLC will keep everything separate, clean, and organized so there's no confusion when it comes to collecting money, making payments, and doing your taxes associated with your rental properties. When it comes to creating your LLC, I also recommend using an attorney for the process and not just going through steps on a website. What you pay a lawyer for their services gains you so much more than just a piece of paper; you get to use their expert knowledge and advice to help you make the best decisions for your business.

Along with a business formation, you'll want to have the proper business insurance in place. It will help to provide coverage and reassurances against any additional items or scenarios surrounding your business, such as any office equipment you might use solely for your business or general liability insurance if someone makes a claim against your business and seeks out compensation. Part of owning a business means making sure it's covered from every angle so that *you're* covered from every angle.

Just because investing in real estate is meant to be a supplemental side gig to your day job doesn't mean you shouldn't take it seriously. Treat it like a business, and in turn, it will show you just how much freedom and gain there is in being in total control of something.

HAVE THE RIGHT MINDSET

Having the right mindset about how to approach this entire endeavor is so important for finding success with it. Not only should you realize that you have a new business on your hands to form and manage, but you need to realize the scope of the full endeavor you're about to undertake. If you're serious about making real estate investing a lucrative side gig for the foreseeable future, you first need to have a mindset of longevity.

Again, reaping big gains from real estate is a long-term task. There's no getting rich quick here, and you can't become frustrated and just give up if you don't automatically start making an extra $10,000 every month. In order to ever potentially get to that point, you have to have the patience and dedication to make it to those long-term destinations.

The setup, research, and purchasing processes all take time. Then, when you have the property in hand and tenants living there, you're going to spend time collecting rent from them month after month, year after year to slowly pay off your mortgage and any other necessary related expenses. The more you scale up the number of properties you rent, the more money will come in, but even so, this is a nice, steady burn. And "steady" is the key here. If you're consistent with the work you put in, the returns you gain will be consistent too. You just have to be ready to maintain that consistency for several years and, sometimes, several decades.

But the trade-off for that time spent, as I've already discussed throughout this book, is that you absolutely have the means to do this without any formal education or training. You can't say the same thing about a lot of other moneymaking gigs. Which brings us to our second important mindset for success: having a can-do attitude.

You have to *believe* that this is something you can do. Because it really and truly is. You might feel like you're on rocky ground, or you might doubt that you can get your finances in order the way you need, but don't let those feelings overtake and derail you. Let "yes I can" rise above all that negative chatter and be your mantra as you start these steps, whatever they may be. Without it, you won't get far. But with it, you can do great things. As Henry Ford said, "Whether you think you can, or you think you can't—you're right."

And finally, similar to treating this like a business, is the mindset of taking the emotion out of it. You will face plenty of emotional moments on this journey: the elation of purchasing your first property, the excitement of fixing it up and making it a desirable place to live, the anxiousness of vetting your first tenants, the awe of seeing your bank statements earning a little more cushion over time. But in order to make the soundest decisions for your business, you have to lead with your head instead of your heart.

I by no means felt *good* about giving that tenant $400 of my hard-earned money to help them move out of my property. But letting those emotions get the best of me would not have been best for my business. I had to take my emotion out of the equation in order to come to a conclusion that worked for everyone and benefited my business in the long run.

There are going to be tough choices to make during this process. On top of being tough, some of them you just plain won't feel good making. But you have to be able to separate your emotions from your decision-making processes if you want to succeed. You might have to be the landlord who bears down on the tenant who hasn't paid rent for two months even though confrontations make you squirm. You might have to squash your excitement over a property's premium location if it's outside your budget. Or you might have to put your disdain over a less-than-desirable property aside if the numbers make the most sense for your goal. Being successful in real estate investing means putting aside your feelings for the greater good of your bottom line—and not just the one you can see right in front of you. You have to keep that long-term mindset and always remember that "can-do" will get you far.

CHAPTER FIVE
WHERE THERE'S A WHY, THERE'S A WAY

AT THE CORE OF THE "AMERICAN DREAM" is the desire to own property, to call a little slice of land on this great big continent your own and to have the freedom to do with it whatever you please. It's an ideal scenario, and it is part of the American dream for a very good reason.

Unfortunately, that dreamscape has shifted in people's minds in recent years. As homeownership, whether for living or renting purposes, has become more expensive, many people take that to mean they have no chance at ever becoming a property owner. And they resign themselves to that belief for their entire lives without considering how to change it.

But that dream is not dead. In fact, it's still alive and thriving—but only if you want it to be. You can own a home to live in, and then some, if you're willing to put in the work it takes and make the sacrifices necessary to get there. For that reason, investing in real estate is not a matter of *if*. It's a matter of *how*.

When exploring options for my first rental property, I had no clue what I was doing, no idea what investing in real estate really meant or what it entailed, and yet I pushed forward with it. Both my wife and my dad—who I turn to for financial advice frequently—told me that it just felt like an inherently bad idea. But something in my gut told me I'd regret it if I didn't at least try. So I found a way to make it work, with no money saved up and minimal cash in the bank. I used a HELOC on my primary residence for the first down payment of 10 percent (generally a down payment on an investment property is 20 percent, but there are many creative ways of financing), and as soon as that first rental was working the way I envisioned, I knew I wanted to scale up what I was doing. And that meant purchasing more rental properties. The problem was, my second rental property was going to require a 20 percent down payment. Now, what was I supposed to do? All the money I was earning on the first property was either paying off the mortgage on it, paying down my line of credit, or being saved for things like maintenance, upkeep, and emergencies for the property.

I was essentially back to square one. That meant it was time to get creative.

My family readjusted our spending and started living more frugally. We spent less on groceries, less on going out, and less on buying frivolous things. I worked double shifts and overtime at the fire station, and any money I earned went right into savings for that 20 percent down payment. I scraped together every penny I could in an effort to make it so that I could keep scaling my real estate business. And eventually, I got there.

It all comes down to how badly you want to make this happen for yourself and what you're willing to sacrifice in order to make it happen. And I know "sacrifice" can be a scary word, but it doesn't have to be. It simply means asking yourself what changes you can and are willing to make to the way you live your life *now* so that you can reap the financial benefits of doing so in the future. I guarantee there's at least one adjustment, and probably more, you can make in your life. It just takes a little deep thinking and creativity to get there. Once you do, you'll be surprised at how easily (and even quickly) you can make the money you need to begin your real estate investment endeavors.

Looking back on that time when I was hustling to save for my second investment property, I didn't have the knowledge I do now. I would have done things differently if I had known better, but hustle and perseverance is always key. Now I know that in order to make the needle fly rather than just move, you have to think in terms of bigger pictures and bigger strokes to paint those pictures.

MAKE BIGGER MOVES WITH YOUR MONEY

If you have a monetary goal you're trying to reach, there are tons of investment and finance gurus out there who will advise you to cut that four-dollar cup of coffee every morning and instead put it into savings. While that might be an easy place to start, when you look at it from a broader perspective, you'll realize that saving four dollars a day five days a week only equates to eighty dollars a month. The reality is, that amount isn't going to change your life. Saving up that way with the intention of eventually having enough money for a down payment on a rental property is going to take you years upon years.

Now, if that's the best adjustment you can make at this time, and you're willing to stick with that slow grind, go for it. You can still get there that way if you have the time and patience, but if you're itching to get things done a little faster, there are *always* bigger options for you to consider. There are always heftier sacrifices you can make to get you to your end goal that much faster. It's all about creativity and a willingness to do whatever it takes.

Take a look at your life and figure out where you do most of your spending. Typically, our biggest expenses in life are our housing and transportation. We spend a lot of money on rent and the things we fill our homes with, and we spend a lot of money on our cars and the payments and insurance that come with them. Again, it's all part of the American dream. But in this case, it's about setting aside one dream for another.

How much do you spend to rent your place every month? How can those costs be diminished? Could you move someone else into your place to help you split your rent in half? Could you move to a different part of town that costs a little less? If you did those things, how much would you be saving? I bet it would be much, *much* more than just eighty dollars a month. Now you might be looking at $500 or $1,000 saved up every single month. That's anywhere from $6,000 to $12,000 a year saved.

The same goes for your car. Are you driving around in the latest model with the highest trim and upgrades, costing you $400, $600, or $1,000 a month to finance or lease? What would happen if you temporarily down-graded to a ten-year-old model that still gets you from point A to point B as needed? What would just an extra $400 a month in your savings be able to do for you? There's an additional $4,800 a year to go on top of the money you're saving by adjusting your living situation.

It's all about sacrifice. *What are you willing to give up now in order to have what you want later?*

And that sacrifice can go even deeper than just finding ways to save money you used to spend. If you can find a way to earn more money at the same time, you can propel yourself toward your goal even faster. Consider sacrificing some of your free time so you can work a couple shifts of overtime a week. Grab a part-time job or research some side gigs you can take on in order to make more money. Then take that additional income and set it aside for your future investment. You might be tired at the end of every week, but it will all be worth it when you're making twice as much money with less than half the work through an investment property.

These are all substantial changes that you have the ability to make. They're going to change your life a whole lot faster than skipping your four-dollar coffee a few times a week will. So think big, then go big.

TURN TO WHAT YOU ALREADY KNOW

I am not afraid to admit that I had no clue what I was doing when I first got into the real estate investment game. It took plenty of confusion, frustration, and trial and error to gain all the knowledge and understanding I needed to be an expert at what I do now. But even though that may have been the case, I wasn't flying blindly into this brand-new venture. There was plenty of other knowledge and experience I already had in different areas of my life when I first started out, and those things absolutely contributed to me being able to turn my real estate side hustle into a lucrative business. And the same is true for you—you likely have an array of skills, processes, and mindsets that you've honed to this point in your life that you might be surprised to find help you become really strong in the world of real estate investing.

Because I was a home inspector well before I purchased my first property, I already possessed inside knowledge of what made a home a good investment from a physical standpoint. It gave me the ability to see the potential in a property, but also helped me to understand what I might be getting myself into if I purchased it. I could better determine what maintenance or repairs might need to be made, which meant I knew early in the process if an investment was worth it. My knowledge as a home inspector helped me to know what questions to ask and what numbers to crunch. It helped me to see what was important to worry about and what wasn't. And these are all elements that have continued to serve me well with every property I've purchased from the very beginning.

Working hand in hand with that, my firefighting background gave me the ability to think calmly and critically so as not to make rash decisions. As a firefighter and paramedic, I can't be panicking while I do my job. That wouldn't help anyone and would likely just get me, my partners, and the people we're trying to assist into even bigger trouble. We are called every day to help people on what's likely one of the worst days of their lives. We can't make it worse. We have to maintain a calm presence and demeanor. Often, we end up acting like life coaches for our patients and the public. My decades of experience with that type of calm control and precise decision-making allows me to bring that same rational and critical-thinking mindset to the real estate work I do. I don't panic when something goes wrong—I break it down into actionable steps that allow me to solve the problem, then I tackle each one with a clear head.

Emergency responders tend to make quick decisions with limited information. For example, upon arriving at a structure fire, we have approximately thirty to forty-five seconds to assess the situation, create a plan of action, request additional resources, and execute the plan. And we do it all with limited information. I've heard from military folks that you only really need 80 percent of the information available in any situation to make an actionable decision. Firefighters rarely have even that percentage at the beginning of an emergency, but we constantly reassess, re-evaluate, and address accordingly.

I've learned that business is the same. If you wait to gain 100 percent of the information before making a decision, it may be a great plan, but it no longer applies, as that particular situation the plan applied to has now passed. So I make calm, rational, and quick decisions. I know no other way to approach life, and I have my fire-fighting background to thank for that.

What do you have in your life that you can rely on to help with your real estate investment goals? It doesn't have to have anything to do with real estate, and it probably won't. If you're a first responder like me, it more likely has to do with your mindset and how you approach obstacles. Whatever it may be, bring it to the surface of your processes, and utilize it any way you can. Use what you already know to your advantage as you try to tackle something you don't know. You'd be amazed by what pockets of useful information you already possess that can help you on this journey.

There's a lot to consider when it comes to jumping into real estate investing for the first time. Before the investing can even begin, you need to find some time to dedicate to soul-searching, researching, planning, and sacrificing. If that sounds like a lot of work, that's because it is—at least, in the beginning. It always takes a hefty dedication of time and energy to start something great. Thankfully, in the case of real estate investing, those start-up processes, if done right, can lead to smooth sailing as you passively collect your additional income. But even then, there will always be work to do, even if you're hiring out a large portion of that work to others. No successful business is *truly* ever completely hands off to the people at the top.

That is, unless you decide to invest in a real estate syndication.

CHAPTER SIX

SYNDICATIONS

YOU MAY HAVE HEARD THE TERM "syndication" before, whether it had to do with real estate or not. That's because in the world of business, you can syndicate just about anything (within certain legal limits). To syndicate something means combining groups or individuals to serve or promote a common interest, usually involving some financial funding or backing of a project. The idea is to pool money from investors together specifically to buy some kind of investment. Then, any returns on that investment are shared between all the investors.

You can syndicate cryptocurrency. You can syndicate oil and gas wells. There are even companies that syndicate ATMs and vending machines, meaning they raise money from investors to purchase and place the machines, run the business of restocking them, and then pay out part of the machines' earnings back to those investors.

Real estate syndications work in much the same way. A real estate syndication pools investments from a variety of backers to purchase, run, and maintain properties. Then part of the earnings from those properties—whether current cash flow earnings or future sale of the property—are paid back to the investors. Not only do the investors get their money back, but the hope (and the reason they invest in the first place) is that they will earn back even more than they invested.

Syndications are a fantastic option for people who want to invest in real estate but don't have the time or desire to put in all the legwork that comes with setting up the processes, vetting and purchasing properties, and running and maintaining those properties. What they do have, however, are the cash reserves to make a meaningful investment. So, as with most things in the game of real estate investing, there are trade-offs and opportunities everywhere.

HOW IT WORKS

In any syndication operation, there are people on the ground running things, and there are people who are strictly investing their money in the operation that's being run by others. We call those two different people "active investors" and "passive investors." Active investors are also often referred to as "general partners," and passive investors are also referred to as "limited partners."

I actually prefer to mix the two options and refer to each party regularly as general partners and passive investors, because it creates a much clearer distinction between them and provides a more accurate description of each person's role.

The general partners are the ones putting the entire deal together, meaning they're setting up the business to run the investments, doing all the property research and vetting, collecting the money, and purchasing and maintaining all the properties. That's why they're considered "active" investors. Often, in addition to the passive investors' money, general partners invest their own money into a property investment, but they also invest their time and energy into getting the work done. Because of this, they have skin in the game.

Passive investors are essentially the opposite. They get to take a look at all the property proposals the general partners have already researched and put together for them, select which ones they would like to invest in, and then send their money over to be invested in their selections. Then they get to sit back and wait for the property to earn its returns. They will receive their portion of those returns from the general partners.

There's no single type of property you should expect a syndication to invest in. In general, however, because investments are being pooled together from various sources, the resulting investment properties tend to be larger or more expensive to purchase up front, because they have the means to make those kinds of purchases. For example, many syndications focus on purchasing large apartment complexes because the larger sum of money from their investors allows them to do so, and the returns can be a lot bigger when you have more units on a single property. But syndications may also focus on investing in single-family homes and smaller multi-family dwellings as well. There are syndications that focus entirely on properties like trailer parks, commercial buildings, hotels, self-storage facilities, medical buildings, and countless others as their investment opportunities.

There are also a lot of different ways a syndication can be set up and operated based on what its primary investors are looking for and what kinds of properties they aim to invest in. Some of them give their investors a general sense of the type of investments they're aiming to make, collect a certain amount of money to that end, and then go and make the investments. Others will already have specific properties in mind and ready to move forward with so the passive investor can directly consider those properties and decide if they want to invest in them. There are even general partners asking investors to trust them enough to fund their general endeavors up front so that they can then go do the legwork of finding the right properties for everyone involved, generally with specific direction in mind. There's no one right or wrong way to do things, and it all depends on the goals and nature of the relationship between the general partners and passive investors.

And though the role of a passive investor in any scenario is much more hands-off, when it comes to real estate, you should never aim to be *completely* passive. In order to make sure they're making sound investment decisions, passive investors should still put some time and thought into both which syndication/general partners they decide to trust and invest with, as well as which properties the syndication has to offer that they will decide to invest in. Granted, passive investors could just choose at random and hope for the best, but as we already know, that's never the best way to go about investing in real estate. How and where you invest your money is all about what your goals and reasons for investing are—even for passive investors.

REASONS TO BE A PASSIVE INVESTOR

As already mentioned, the primary reason someone would likely choose to be a passive investor rather than a general partner is because they don't have the time, energy, or desire to do all the legwork required to continuously research and purchase new rental properties. They also may just not have the level of knowledge (or the time to gain it) they would prefer to have for making these types of investment decisions themselves.

But there are plenty of other reasons beyond "I just don't want to" for a passive investor to decide to invest in real estate this way. And they should be looking for general partners who have set up their syndication to match those reasons and goals.

For example, if someone is a high-net-worth earner, like a doctor or a lawyer, they may not be concerned about getting the highest monthly returns on their real estate investments because they really don't need the extra cash flow. Instead, they might want an investment that helps them with their taxes. Remember, if you own real estate, there are certain tax benefits and write-offs that come with it that can help to reduce the amount of taxes you owe each year. So these kinds of passive investors may just be looking for the right properties and contracts that will give them those benefits—ones that their salaried careers don't give them. In that case, their requirement for investing with a specific syndication may be to take a larger portion of the tax advantages on the property and to sacrifice some of their returns.

On the other hand, other investors, who might not be as high of earners, but still have enough reserves to make some initial investments into properties, may instead be looking for that additional monthly cash flow and are less concerned with the tax consequences of that fact. So they might be more than happy with earning their straight returns on their investments and having that cash flow to do with whatever they would like.

Not every syndication is right for every type of investor. Much like the person who wants to purchase and manage rental properties all on their own, before you can make the investment, you should do some deep thinking about the Why behind the decision so you have a clearer path forward for getting there.

QUALIFICATIONS FOR INVESTING IN SYNDICATIONS

You might be wondering why the first five chapters of this book detailed all the ways you can and should go into business for yourself as a hands-on real estate investor when all along there's been an option to just trust someone else with your money and have them do all the work for you.

Well, the reason is that not everyone can be a passive investor in every type of real estate syndication. There are certain qualifying parameters that these investors are required to meet in order to be able to invest in certain deals. And this is because there are very specific larger legal parameters that syndications themselves are required to adhere to if they want to stay in business and operate freely.

To start, a syndication—real estate or otherwise— falls under the US Securities and Exchange Commission's

(SEC) definition of a "security." That definition states that something is a security when money is raised and the return is generated by the sponsors' efforts without input from the investors. In other words, a business is a security when the people putting the money into the company have no say about how the company decides to use that money to generate returns for everyone involved.

All securities must be legally registered with the SEC, which means they become publicly traded companies, unless one of the specific SEC rule exemptions is used to not be publicly traded. The vast majority of real estate syndications, and syndications in general, use one or more of the SEC rule exemptions to avoid being publicly traded. But that doesn't mean they just get a free pass to run the syndication however they would like. It means there are other sets of rules they must adhere to and maintain in order to keep themselves within those exemptions. Otherwise, they must go public or risk being an illegal entity.

There are some very specific regulations dictating how a real estate syndication's general partners must file notice of property purchases and sales in order to stay exempt, and these details are coordinated by an attorney familiar with SEC rules. But the important details for you to know and understand are the ones that directly affect you as a potential investor, and they have to do with how a syndication raises its capital.

REGULATION 506 D exemptions are the most popular type of real estate syndication, and they can:

- Raise unlimited capital
- Raise money from an unlimited number of accredited investors who must verify their own accreditation
- Raise money from a maximum of thirty-five nonaccredited investors
- Not advertise their syndication in any way and must instead have a pre-existing substantive relationship with investors

REGULATION 506 C syndications can:

- Only accept investments from accredited investors and must take specific steps to verify each investor's accreditation themselves
- Advertise their syndication publicly

REGULATION A+ syndications can:

- Accept capital from nonaccredited investors, but any such investment must be in an amount no more than 10 percent of an individual's net worth
- Advertise their syndication publicly
- Raise a maximum of $75 million
- Face a specific filing process with the SEC that takes additional time

So what, exactly, do all these details mean for you? It depends on whether you qualify as an accredited investor or not. To qualify as an accredited investor, you must have a net worth of at least $1 million, excluding your primary residence. You must also have earned $200,000 in income over the last two years and have a reasonable expectation of doing so in the current year. If you have a spouse, that number changes to $300,000. If you fall outside any of those parameters, you are considered a nonaccredited investor.

The reason accredited investors are given access to certain investments is that the SEC and our US government in general believe that if someone has obtained the above financial minimums, they are savvy enough to invest in unregulated opportunities. Publicly traded stocks, bonds, mutual funds, investment accounts, and retirement accounts, on the other hand, are highly regulated. Some of the risk in those cases has been scrubbed, so it has that upside.

Now, the numbers associated with being an accredited investor might seem like some large numbers to achieve, but they're certainly not impossible. That's what this book is all about, after all—becoming a millionaire firefighter (or other). Until you reach that point, the good news is that even if you're nonaccredited according to the SEC's guidelines, you still have options for investing in syndications. They're just a bit more limited, and therefore, a bit more competitive to secure.

And if and when you become accredited (or if perhaps you already are), then you have an array of syndication opportunities to consider and explore.

Regulation 506D does allow for up to thirty-five nonaccredited to participate in syndications.

WHAT TO LOOK FOR IN A GENERAL PARTNER

I could have called this section "What to Look for in a Syndication," but we already know that the type of syndication you decide to invest in relies heavily on your own finances and ability to contribute certain investment amounts. So really, if you already know what kinds of syndications you qualify for, the next step is determining which of the available offerings is the one you should actually go with. And to best determine that, you need to look closely at the general partners who are running the business.

Once you have some syndication options in place that match your accreditation status and ability to invest, you have to take a closer look at the people behind the business. This isn't the kind of operation where you want to just hand thousands of dollars to the first man in a suit on the street who tells you he has a real estate syndication opportunity for you. Sure, you might get lucky, but is this really the kind of thing you want to leave up to luck? Even as a passive investor, you're here to make your own luck. Once you make it, that's when you can sit back and relax while the returns come in.

To start, make sure the general partners have a good business track record. How long have they been in business? How many properties have they invested in? How many investors do they already have working with them? Do they have reliable references? When you look up their names, do dozens of different associated business entities pop up that seem odd, or is their portfolio generally more focused and related to their syndication work? Does their investing website also talk about their lawn mowing business? If it does, that's not the best sign that they're serious about their investing business.

If their business dealings look good and reliable, next look at the more "human" side of things. If you know them personally already, are they people you generally get along with? Would you feel good about going into business with them? If they're an acquaintance or someone you learned about by word of mouth, ask the person who introduced you to them about them. Pick their brain about what they think about these partners as people. And don't be afraid to check out their various social media profiles to see what kinds of things they're posting and if you align with their opinions and positions. Is their Facebook page or other social media profile full of negative posts whining about needing more money from people because life just isn't fair? That kind of content is a solid red flag. In general, you should feel comfortable on at least some kind of personal level with the person you're going to invest with.

Next, speak with them directly to learn more about how they operate. During these conversations, take note of whether they welcome your questions with ease and if they provide adequate answers to your questions. *Can they answer all your questions?* If not, they may not know their business very well. And if they're less than forthcoming with their answers rather than being open and excited to share more information with you, that could also be a red flag indicating something they don't want you to know about. Or perhaps it could mean they're not interested in you as an investor, which would make them someone you shouldn't want to work with anyway.

On the other hand, if they overwhelm you with complicated investor or real estate jargon and make it difficult for you to even understand what they're talking about, that may not be the best type of business relationship. Similarly, your general partners will understand that you may want to be hands-off as a passive investor, but they shouldn't take that as an opportunity to avoid educating you when you ask for insights.

Also be sure to ask them how they work with their investors. How often do they send new properties to consider? How often do they keep their pool of investors updated on how their investments are going? Also, *how* do they send these updates? Via email? Phone call? Text? How often do they pay out returns to their investors? And are you comfortable with these types of touch points and the frequency with which they will happen?

Who you choose to invest with comes down to your own feelings of trust and your personal comfort level. You have to be able to trust the strength of their business, and you need to be comfortable with the person or people running that business. Though this is a serious invest-ment, you still want to enjoy the ride. Picking the right people to take that ride with will make all the difference.

At this point, I know what you're probably thinking that for a "passive" option for investing in real estate, syndications sound like a lot of work. But like I said earlier, anything worth doing is going to take at least *some* effort at some point during the process. If it didn't, everyone would be taking advantage of the opportuni-ties available out there.

As a passive investor, your heaviest workload comes when picking the right people to invest with. If you make that choice wisely, then you really and truly will get to be as passive as you'd like to be, because you can trust that your general partners are acting in your best interest. But if you're still unsure about where to start or who to look for, don't worry! I know a guy who's here to help.

CHAPTER SEVEN

MY SYNDICATION AND YOUR OPPORTUNITIES

MY WORK AS A REAL ESTATE INVESTOR has been an incredible journey. I'm so thankful for it because it's what allows and will continue to allow me to live my life the way I want today, tomorrow, and well into the future.

But another wonderful thing that has come out of this work for me over the last decade is the ability to work with others who also want to use real estate investments to achieve their own goals. I've been presented with the unique and humbling opportunity to help others discover how real estate investing can change their lives. That's the very reason I decided to write this book: to show others just how doable this is, no matter who you are or where you are in life.

There's so much excitement and power in running your own real estate investment business from the front end to the back end, and I'll always believe it's something anyone can do. But if you've got money you're itching to invest, there's also a lot of benefit to having someone else do all the legwork for you. It all relates back to your Why and figuring out the how for achieving it.

I started my own real estate syndication alongside a highly experienced partner so that we can offer opportunities to all kinds of people interested in investing in real estate. I, of course, love the notion of growing my own investments and portfolio, but this has presented itself as another opportunity for me to include others who may not have the access, knowledge, or desire to make real estate investments on their own. Our syndication is my way of letting everyone know that they always have options to explore.

THE WHOLE IS GREATER THAN THE SUM

I love the saying, "the whole is greater than the sum of its parts." It's such a perfect way to speak about how real estate syndication works and the true power behind it. It's a philosophy I bring to every investment opportunity I present.

Real estate syndications are a team sport, and they're so much better for it. We can all accomplish so much more by working together than if we attempted to achieve the same goals completely on our own. That's not to say you can't reach these kinds of goals on your own, but I truly believe you open a whole new world of possibilities when you work with a great syndication group.

To make a long explanation short, with syndications, investors gain access to properties they wouldn't otherwise be able to, and general partners have the means to present those opportunities to them and reap the additional benefits from that setup. Together, we can do more. Together, there's even more room to grow. Together, we can make this process work.

That's part of the reason I didn't go into my own syndication business alone. I've brought in an incredible partner whose business operations and values align with mine, but their different background brings so much more to the table than I could have offered on my own. By combining our expertise, we expand our capabilities, which means we expand our opportunities.

This person's values align with mine because they are a retired firefighter. And their expertise brings even more to the table than mine does because they also work as a real estate agent. They have so much to offer in areas that are both familiar and eye opening to me that I couldn't contain my excitement when the opportunity to work together arose. And now I'm so excited to bring those opportunities to you.

Our goal is to build an incredible network of reliable and lucrative partnerships that benefit everyone involved. We're not in this to look out for ourselves; we're in it to look out for everyone, because we're nothing without the team supporting us. We realize that, and it's what makes us so eager to do that work.

WHERE WE'LL BE INVESTING

My partner and I have the combined years of experience and knowledge to be smart about where to invest and what to invest in. And we bring that knowledge directly to our investors so they can feel at ease about who they're investing their hard-earned money with.

Our primary focus is on multifamily housing primarily located in areas with positive economic statistics, net in-migration, job creation, industry, landlord-friendly laws and statutes, and places where people just generally want to be. Right now, these areas tend to be the South and the mid-Atlantic areas, but trends constantly change, and adjustments are made accordingly. We made that choice first and foremost because there are preferable economics in those areas, meaning that the population is generally increasing year over year. There are more people regularly moving to those areas than there are moving out of those areas, and that's exactly where you want to have rental properties so that your potential pool of renters for your properties doesn't dry up. And our expectation is that the economy will continue to grow in these areas, meaning there will be more and more people living there who are willing and able to pay rent for their homes.

In these states and their respective counties there also tends to be more favorable landlord laws. When thinking about making large or long-term rental property investments with an eye on what's best for your business, you ideally want to purchase properties that favor the rights of landlords instead of tenants. Otherwise, it can make it more difficult to operate your properties the way you need to. For example, when it comes to the legalities and processes of evicting a problem tenant, some states in other parts of the country make it much more labor-intensive to do so than states in northern areas. And that's not to say we aim to be ruthless with our tenants, not by a long shot. It just means we have better options to choose from when complicated business decisions might need to be made.

Our reason for focusing on multifamily housing over single-family housing goes back to the concept that there will always be a need for housing in places with growing populations. And on multifamily properties like apartment complexes, there are simply more opportunities to offer that housing. There's also less administrative cost and time when you buy a single property with multiple units attached to it. In other words, the same amount of up-front work tends to go into purchasing either a single-family or a multifamily property, so we're playing it smart by making those individual purchases as valuable as possible. Doing so means buying more units for fewer transactions.

It's also easier to scale up with multifamily housing. When you buy a single-family home, you're generally purchasing the house and a yard. You can really only rent to one renter with that property because there's just less rentable space on that property than there is if you're buying a multifamily building. In that case, you're purchasing a piece of property with more than one dwelling unit, which means you're already at an advantage of scaling up to bringing in more renters, meaning more sources of return on your initial investment.

Of course, the trade-off for purchasing larger multifamily properties is that your up-front costs are larger. That's always going to be the case for multifamily housing in comparison to single-family homes. But once again, that's the beauty of syndication: By teaming up together, we can make these large purchases and we can all reap the benefits of doing so.

OUR EXPERIENCE AND VALUES SET US APART

Real estate syndications are an incredible investment opportunity and way of making passive income and generating long-term wealth. For that reason, there are literally hundreds of people who wake up every day and say, "I feel like starting a real estate syndication today."

They might have listened to a podcast or two about it or seen an advertisement and done a little back-end digging. They might have explored the surface level of what it takes to create and run a syndication and thought, *Sure, I can do that.*

And those are exactly the type of general partners you want to avoid.

Instead, you want to work with a syndication that brings experience, knowledge, and integrity to everything it does. You need general partners who have been around the block with real estate investments more than a few times, who have seen their share of success and have also learned plenty from their failures. You want someone who cares about the people they work with and not just finding a way to play around with other people's money.

You want someone like my partner and me.

Our common background in the world of firefighting and being public-service employees gives us the work ethic needed to do this job the right way. We get our job done—and done right—no matter the time of day or what the weather is, because if we don't, it affects so many more people than just us. We are of the mindset that the only thing that matters is the mission, and that's been ingrained in us, no matter if we're fighting fires or purchasing rental properties.

There's plenty you can learn from podcasts and online videos, but nothing compares to real-life experience.

And my partner and I have it in droves. Our combined experiences, not only with purchasing and managing investment properties but with other related backgrounds such as home inspections and real estate sales from an agent's perspective, give us an upper technical hand on all things real estate. We know a good deal when we see one, because we've worked the jobs and made the purchases that taught us those lessons.

Above all of that, however, are the values we hold ourselves to. We run this like a business, but we do it with an understanding that this is a people-centric venture. This is the business of working with people on the back end so that we can make homes available for other people on the front end. And we don't take that responsibility lightly.

When it comes to working with our passive investors, we firmly believe in open communication. That's because the best decisions are made when everyone involved has the education they need to make decisions that feel right for them. We don't just stroll up to people with our palms out asking for cash. In fact, there are plenty of interested investors who we sometimes turn away because the personable and reliable fit just isn't there—no matter how much money they might be offering up as incentive. We take time to really connect with our investors, learn what they're looking to achieve with their investment, and share how our business ethics and dealings might be exactly what they're looking for.

We're clear about our processes, expectations, and results, taking care to let our investors know what's what no matter how well an investment might (or might not) be doing. We celebrate the highs together, and we share our rethinking and re-strategizing about possible lows. We don't hide behind big jargon, and we don't spring surprises. Our leadership philosophy is that everyone involved in a business venture together has a right to know as much or as little as they might like.

If a property is performing well, we share why that is with regular updates. If a property isn't performing the way we had initially hoped, we share that fact outright, and then we let them know what we're going to do to fix it. Because once again, our team is mission focused; we don't stop until the job is done right.

I could talk about my own real estate syndication until I'm blue in the face because I love it and the work I do with people every day. But the reality is, you have many different options to explore if you decide that investing in a syndication as a passive partner is your best path forward over investing in your own property directly.

There are different types of syndications, investor levels, and properties to consider. There are different businesses and partners to take into account. There are fountains of information available to you in a variety of formats all about this business and what it can do for you. I encourage you to explore your options and see what really and truly fits best with your life and your goals.

But when making your decision, I urge you to always keep in mind the people behind the decisions to come. Look at them closely in every way I've described to you. They are going to be the decision that matters most. Who you put your faith and trust in is imperative when it comes to being successful with investing in real estate syndications. The right people make all the difference.

CHAPTER EIGHT

YOU CAN DO THIS

YOU KNOW WHAT I LOVE about real estate investing the most? Anyone can do it. When it comes to a lot of other moneymaking and wealth-building ventures, there are so many massive barriers to entry that they are hard to overcome. They might require years of schooling or experience to even think about getting started. Or they might require hundreds of thousands of dollars put in up front just to try to get the ball rolling. Sometimes, they even require dropping everything you love and making a total career shift in order to make room for whatever it is you're hoping to make money by doing instead.

But that's not the case with real estate investing. You don't need to enroll in school—you can self-educate to start. You don't need massive piles of cash to purchase your first single-family home—you just need to save up enough for a down payment. And you don't need to quit your career or the hobbies you love in order to focus on real estate exclusively—once you figure out the ropes, the process can almost run itself. And that's especially true if you invest in syndications.

For all those reasons and more, real estate investing can be an opportunity for everyone. And that's why I love it. It's also the reason I'm able to do it. When I got started, I had no formal education, training, or even deeper knowledge about how things in the real estate world worked. I was just a blue-collar, frontline firefighter who saw the potential in this strange new world. I promise, I started right where you are now, and I've come so far. I've made myself into a millionaire firefighter by doing the deep digging and hard work that it takes to get there. But *anyone* can do that same kind of hard work. And if they don't want to, there are *still* other options to explore. Real estate really is incredible that way, and that's why I'll never stop trying to connect with others about it.

Hopefully by now, you'll have come to understand just how doable this process is for yourself too. You'll have learned how many different options you have for getting started. You'll have seen how making just a few changes now can lead to incredible and reliable results later.

It's never too early or too late to start when it comes to real estate. I've worked with people who are eighty years old when they decide to buy their first investment property so they can leave it to a family member and help them take advantage of certain tax situations. I've worked with young adults—one of the youngest being my own daughter, at nineteen years old, who already has a few investment properties—and they see the value in starting to build their wealth early in life. And I've worked with every type of person of every age in between who has decided to start on this exciting journey because they finally saw and understood not only how doable this is but how lucrative it can be.

There are no age restrictions here. There aren't even any class, knowledge, or time restrictions. The only restriction is your mindset. The only thing that can hold you back is how you decide to think about and approach investing in real estate. You are your only barrier to entry. But if you equip yourself with the right mindset, you build yourself a ladder to get right up and over that barrier. Stepping on that first rung is your decision to make, though. No one can make it for you. You have to find your own reason to start, and your own motivation to actually take that first step.

Think back to the chapter about your Why. What's the reason you want to do this? What's the reason you want to get involved in real estate investing? What change do you want it to bring to your life? How do you want that change to impact you and your family? Figure that out, and let it fuel you.

Then do that self-education. Figure out what road best leads to your Why and how you can most feasibly navigate that road. Decide if running your own ship is the best course forward or if investing with a partner who does the heavy lifting for you might be best for you and your current lifestyle or situation. If you're going to take the reigns and be your own investor and manager, ingest all the information you can about it. This book is a great starting place. Now, what other resources are out there for you to take advantage of? What other books can you read? What podcasts can you listen to? What seminars or workshops can you attend? What master-mind groups can you join so that you're surrounded by like-minded individuals who want to succeed in the same way you do and will inspire you to that end?

If you're interested in syndications and being a passive investor, take a look at your finances. What kind of investor can you be? What kinds of syndications are available for you to invest in? And where can you meet general partners so you can get to know them better and determine who feels like the right one to invest with?

Don't be afraid to ask yourself questions that will not only lead to insightful answers but will actually open the door for more and more questions to come through. Don't ever stop learning and growing that way. Be hungry with curiosity about how you can better your life through real estate, and it will serve you back tenfold. I've been doing this for well over a decade now and have never stopped seeking out education. I'm part of the masterminds and seminars that happen every month; I sit in on the classes with experts who know more than I do. And I constantly have a podcast or an audiobook about some kind of real estate, leadership, or business topic playing in the background of my life. There's so much to learn here, and that's part of what makes it so exciting.

I don't foresee my involvement in the world of real estate investing ever really diminishing in any way. I unfortunately can't say the same thing about being a firefighter; at some point, when I've dedicated all the time and energy that my body can afford to being a frontline worker in that way, I will retire. That's the way that all firefighting careers go, no matter how much we might love them and want to continue with them. And no matter how true that is, I will always think of myself a firefighter, even long after my days of fighting flames are over.

Real estate investing, on the other hand, doesn't necessarily need to go the same way. I meant it when I said there don't have to be any age restrictions here; it's never too late to get started, let alone keep going. It's something that can be as hands-off or hands-on as you make it, and I don't see myself sitting around in front of a TV for the majority of my retirement. No, the call of real estate investing will always pull me toward it in some form or fashion, and I know the nature of how it works will allow me to keep participating in it however I might like. It's just another one of the perks I've come to discover and love about this industry.

Where do you see yourself five years from now? How about ten? Twenty? Are you still working in the career you've built much of your life around? And is that what you still want to be doing? If so, that's fantastic. But now look a little closer. Is that career helping you live the life you envision for yourself? Is it giving you the means to know you'll be okay well after the time comes to leave that career? If it is, you're doing things right, so keep it up! But if it's not . . . well, the one key takeaway I hope you've gained after reading this book is that an option exists out there that *can* help you live exactly the life you'd love when you reach that point.

It all comes down to how willing and ready you are to take your own destiny into your own hands. There's no luck to wait around for, no handouts to expect, and no time like the present. This is about making your own luck, no longer relying on others to get you ahead in life, and realizing that there will never be a better time to invest in real estate. Because the sooner you start, the sooner you'll reap the incredible payoff it has the power to provide. But that's only if you're ready to make things happen.

Step out of your "I'm just a blue-collar worker" mindset. Stop telling yourself "I'll never be able to do this." Don't be afraid to take the plunge. If you're like me and currently work as a firefighter, police officer, nurse, teacher, or in another position that makes sacrifices for and directly serves your community, then you already take plunges every day. You put yourself on the line to help others. You tackle challenges and risks that other people have no interest in. You're doing hard work already. It's time to make your hard work, work for you in return. It's time to explore how real estate investing can give you the life you and your family deserve, without having to give up the work you already know and love. It is so very possible if you want it to be.

INDEX OF
REAL ESTATE TERMS

ACTIVE INVESTOR (OR GENERAL PARTNER): In a real estate syndication, the active investor/general partner directly runs the operations of the syndication business, from researching and presenting properties to investors to collecting investments and purchasing and managing properties.

ADJUSTABLE-RATE MORTGAGE (ARM): A mortgage with an interest rate that can change periodically based on market conditions.

AMORTIZATION: The process of gradually paying off a mortgage loan through regular payments, typically monthly.

APPRAISAL: An evaluation of a property's value conducted by a professional appraiser.

APPRAISAL CONTINGENCY: A clause that allows a buyer to cancel a purchase agreement if a home's appraised value is found to be less than the sale price.

APPRECIATION: The value a property naturally gains over time as general home values rise.

ASSESSED VALUE: The value assigned to a property for taxation purposes by a government authority.

ASSUMPTION: When a buyer takes over the seller's existing mortgage on the property.

BUYER'S MARKET: A market condition in which there are more properties for sale than there are buyers, usually giving buyers an advantage with purchasing power and price negotiation.

CAPITALIZATION RATE: The rate of return on an investment property based on its net operating income.

CERTIFICATE OF TITLE: A document that certifies the ownership of a property and confirms that there are no liens or encumbrances on it.

CLOSING: The final stage of a real estate transaction when the property is transferred from the seller to the buyer.

CLOSING COSTS: The fees and expenses associated with the purchase or sale of a property, such as title insurance, appraisal fees, and legal fees.

CONDO: Short for "condominium," a type of housing where individuals own a unit within a larger building or community.

CONTINGENCY: A condition that must be met for a real estate contract to become binding, such as the buyer obtaining financing or a satisfactory inspection.

CONVENTIONAL SALE: When a property is owned outright (or has no mortgage remaining) or the owner owes less on their mortgage than what the market indicates they could sell it for.

CONVEYANCE: The transfer of ownership of a property from one party to another.

COVENANTS, CONDITIONS, AND RESTRICTIONS (CC AND RS): Rules and regulations places on a property by the HOA, developer, or builder that sets forth any requirements or limitations of what a homeowner is allowed to do with their property, including any monthly/annual fees that may be due as an HOA member.

DEBT-TO-INCOME RATIO: A number used by mortgage lenders to determine affordability based on their available loan programs, which also helps them to estimate how much a buyer can afford to pay monthly for a mortgage.

DEED: A legal document that transfers ownership of a property from one party to another.

DEPRECIATION: The decrease in the value of a property over time, often due to wear and tear or obsolescence.

DOWN PAYMENT: The initial payment made by a buyer toward the purchase of a property, typically a percentage of the total purchase price.

EARNEST MONEY: A deposit made by the buyer to demonstrate their serious intent to purchase the property. Sometimes also called a "good faith deposit."

EQUITY: The value of a property that exceeds any outstanding mortgage or loan balance.

ESCROW: A neutral third party that holds funds or documents during a real estate transaction until certain conditions are met.

ESCROW HOLDER: The impartial, third-party agent/depositary who collects the money, documents, personal property, and other items of value to be held until closing on a property is complete.

FAIR MARKET VALUE: The price at which a property would sell between a willing buyer and a willing seller, both under no compulsion to buy or sell.

FHA LOAN: Part of a group of loans that are insured by the federal government. The FHA ensures banks and private lenders that they will cover losses incurred in the event the borrower does not repay the loan in full or on time. Generally, only first-time homebuyers qualify for an FHA loan.

FIXED-RATE MORTGAGE: A mortgage with an interest rate that remains the same for the entire term of the loan, often available as a ten, fifteen, twenty, or thirty-year loan.

FORECLOSURE: The legal process through which a lender takes possession of a property when the borrower fails to make mortgage payments.

HOME INSPECTION: A professional evaluation of a property's condition, typically performed before a purchase is complete.

HOMEOWNERS ASSOCIATION (HOA): An organization that sets rules and regulations for a community or condominium complex, typically collecting fees from residents to cover maintenance and shared expenses.

HOMEOWNERS INSURANCE: Insurance coverage that protects the owner against property damage and liability risks.

HVAC: An acronym for heating, ventilation, and air conditioning, which every home contains in some form, making it an important item to examine closely when considering a property for purchase.

INTEREST RATE: The proportion of a mortgage loan that is charged as interest to the borrower as "payment" for borrowing the loan amount from the lender. Interest rates can be fixed or adjustable for the life of the loan.

LIEN: A legal claim or encumbrance on a property, typically as security for the repayment of a debt.

LISTING: A property that is officially for sale and available on the market.

MARKET ANALYSIS: An assessment of current market conditions to determine property values and trends.

MARKET VALUE: The price at which a property is likely to sell based on current market conditions.

MORTGAGE: A loan used to finance the purchase of a property, with the property serving as collateral.

MULTIFAMILY PROPERTY: A rental property that consists of a multiple-dwelling unit on the property—such as duplex, fourplex, or multiple apartment units—where more than a single renter can live on the property at any one time.

MULTIPLE LISTING SERVICE (MLS): A database that real estate agents use to share information about properties available for sale.

OFFER/COUNTEROFFER: A proposal from a buyer to purchase a property at a specified price and terms, and the seller's response offer to that initial offer.

OPEN HOUSE: An event where a property is available for viewing by potential buyers without an appointment.

PASSIVE INVESTOR (OR LIMITED PARTNER):
In a real estate syndication, the passive investor/ limited partner invests a monetary amount as their contribution to the investment property and has no additional input into how the syndication business or its properties are run or managed.

PREAPPROVAL: The process in which a lender evaluates a borrower's financial situation and creditworthiness to determine the maximum loan amount they can receive.

PREQUALIFICATION: A lender's estimate of the amount a buyer can expect to be approved for during the loan process, not usually based on any hard proof or financial verifications.

PRINCIPAL: The original amount of money borrowed in a mortgage loan, excluding interest.

PROPERTY TAX: A tax imposed by local government authorities based on the assessed value of a property.

PURCHASE/SALE AGREEMENT: A legal contract outlining the terms and conditions of a property sale between the buyer and seller.

REAL ESTATE AGENT: A licensed professional who represents buyers or sellers in real estate transactions.

REAL ESTATE BROKER: A licensed professional who can own a brokerage and supervise other agents.

REAL ESTATE INVESTMENT: The purchase of property with the goal of generating income or appreciation.

RENT-BACK: An arrangement whereby the buyer, who is the new homeowner, agrees to allow the seller, the now-tenant, to stay in the house beyond the close of escrow as needed, but according to pre-set terms between the two parties.

SELLER CONCESSION: An offering a seller may present to buyers in an effort to incentivize the buyer to purchase the home. For example, it could be a contribution toward the buyer's closing costs.

SELLER FINANCING: When the seller provides financing to the buyer instead of or in addition to a traditional mortgage.

SELLER'S MARKET: A market condition in which there are more buyers than available properties for sale, usually giving sellers an advantage with price negotiation.

SHORT SALE: An offer on a property at an asking price that is less than the amount due on the current owner's mortgage. Usually, the homeowner who agrees to a short sale is under financial distress and needs to sell the property to avoid foreclosure or greater value loss on the property.

SINGLE-FAMILY PROPERTY: A rental property that consists of a single unit—such as a house, townhome, or condominium—with only a single renter or single renting entity in that unit, such as an individual person or a single family.

SURVEY: A professional measurement and mapping of a property's boundaries and features.

SYNDICATION: A method of pooling capital from multiple investors for the common goal of acquiring real estate, usually used to purchase properties that are significantly larger than any one investor could afford on their own.

TITLE: A legal document that proves ownership of a property.

TITLE INSURANCE: Insurance that protects against financial loss due to defects in the title or ownership of a property.

TITLE SEARCH: An examination of public records to verify the legal ownership of a property and uncover any potential issues or claims.

UNDER CONTRACT: A stage in the home buying process where the buyer and seller have reached a mutual agreement on the terms of the sale, but the transaction is not yet complete.

VA LOAN: A Department of Veteran Affairs loan, which is guaranteed by the federal government and available to military members, both active and retired, as well as to some eligible spouses. It can include a low or no down payment with competitive rates and fees.

ABOUT THE AUTHOR

GREG CLATTERBUCK has been a career firefighter and paramedic for over twenty years, having earned the rank of lieutenant. He is also the founder of Clatterbuck Home Inspections, which provides inspections for hundreds of homes in Virginia every year. His experience as a real estate investor and the founding of his real estate syndication, Career Capital, have led to the purchase and ownership of dozens of single-family and multifamily rental properties, enabling him to build his worth to over one million dollars in just one short decade.

Greg currently lives in the same town he grew up in rural Virginia with his wife and teenage daughter. He's proud to say that his endeavors have inspired his daughter to purchase two of her own investment properties at the young age of nineteen.

To learn more about Greg, the real estate mastermind groups he's a member of or how you might be able to get involved with his syndication, follow him on:

LINKEDIN

https://www.linkedin.com/in/greg-clatterbuck-87b2ab23

FACEBOOK

https://m.facebook.com/people/Greg-Clatterbuck/100010900117577

WEBSITE

FFCareerCapital.com